T 6902

CENTER STAGE

BILL COSBY

By
William Sanford
Carl Green

Edited By
Dr. Howard Schroeder
Professor in Reading and Language Arts
Dept. of Elementary Education
Mankato State University

Produced & Designed By
Baker Street Productions, Ltd.

CRESTWOOD HOUSE

Mankato, Minnesota
U.S.A.

LIBRARY OF CONGRESS CATALOGING IN PUBLICATION DATA

Sanford, William R. (William Reynolds), 1927 -
Bill Cosby : America's favorite funny man.

(Center stage)
Bibliography: p.
SUMMARY: A biography of a popular comedian, star of his own television show.
1. Cosby, Bill, 1937-   —Juvenile literature. 2. Entertainers—United States—
Biography—Juvenile Literature. [1. Cosby, Bill, 1937-   . 2. Comedians. 3. Afro-
Americans—Biography] I. Green, Carl R. II. Title. III. Series.
PN2287.C632S26   1986   792.7'028'0924 [B] [92]   86-16544
ISBN 0-89686-297-6

International Standard Book Number: 0-89686-297-6	**Library of Congress Catalog Card Number:** 86-16544

ILLUSTRATION CREDITS:

Cover: Gary Gershoff/Retna
Nick Elgar/LGI: 5, 9
UPI/Bettmann Newsphotos: 11, 19, 22
Gary Gershoff/Retna: 13, 14, 30-31
Vinnie Zuffante/Star File: 17
AP/Wide World Photos: 21, 29
Angie Coqueran/LGI: 25
Robert Roth/LGI: 26

CRESTWOOD HOUSE

Hwy. 66 South, Box 3427
Mankato, MN 56002-3427
507-388-1616

TABLE
OF
CONTENTS

INTRODUCTION

Is there anyone who doesn't love Bill Cosby?

Three hundred wet, happy people crowd into the Brooklyn, New York television studio. Rain is falling outside, but no one cares. They all feel lucky, like lottery winners. This old studio is the home of the *Bill Cosby Show.*

To Cosby's fans, the set looks like the home of a trusted friend. A girl pokes her sister and whispers, "Bill wanted the set to look just like his own house in Manhattan. See the pictures on the walls? They're copies of his favorite paintings."

The talking stops when the master of ceremonies (MC) walks onto the set. The MC's job is to "warm up" the audience with some jokes. The jokes are not all good, but no one seems to mind. Finally, the MC introduces the actors. The five Huxtable "kids" and Bill's "TV wife" draw loud applause. "Where's Bill?" someone yells.

All at once, he's there. Bill Cosby waves and gives

Bill Cosby is America's favorite father.

his famous smile. Some people stand and clap for him. This is "Cos," America's favorite father. At last, they sit down. The director signals for the taping to start.

The script calls for a twenty-two minute program. Taping takes much longer, however. It takes time to set up lights and move cameras. Other delays come when Bill thinks a line isn't getting a good laugh. He makes changes on the spot. A few scenes have to be reshot when the actors "goof" their lines. Bill isn't amused. At one point, one of the girls forgets the same line twice. Bill stares at her and snaps, "Get it together!"

The famous Cosby humor shows up, too. Five-year-old Keshia Knight, who plays Rudy, gets tired of waiting. Bill seems to understand. He fills in the time by showing her how to dance the boogaloo. She begins doing the steps, with Bill dancing along behind her. His big body seems to be made of rubber. The audience laughs and cheers.

When the taping is over, Bill looks for his wife. Camille is sitting in the first row. He blows her a kiss. Perhaps he's thinking of how far they've come since he was a poor kid growing up in Philadelphia, Pennsylvania.

CHAPTER ONE

Growing up poor in Philadelphia

William Henry Cosby, Jr., was born in Philadelphia on July 12, 1937. After Bill came James, Russell, and Robert. William and Anna Cosby lived in a housing project. Like their neighbors, the Cosbys were poor. Unable to find a good job, William left to join the Navy.

William sent money home, but it wasn't enough. Anna had to work twelve hours a day to take care of her boys. When times were really bad, the family had to go on welfare. Even so, the Cosby boys always had warm clothes and enough to eat.

Anna was a strong person. Bill says that she taught him right from wrong. Some of the boys in the project ended up in jail. But Bill loved his mother too much to hurt her by getting into trouble. He had already seen his mother cry. Bill's brother, James, died when Bill was only eight years old.

Somehow, Anna found the time to read to the boys at night. She read the Bible, and the funny stories of Mark Twain. Today, Bill believes there's a lot of Twain's famous humor in his own way of telling a story.

Anna was also Bill's first audience. He had a gift for making up stories that made her laugh.

A nine-year-old worker

Bill started work when he was only nine years old. His first job was shining shoes on the street. Two years later, he found summer work in a grocery store. He worked twelve hours a day for only eight dollars (US) a week.

Whenever he was free, Bill played sports with his friends. The boys played football and stickball on the streets. Even while he was having fun, Bill was storing up memories. Today, some of his best stories come from those street games. Fat Albert, Weird Harold, and Crying Charlie are his names for some of his old friends.

The kid who makes people laugh

Bill clowned his way through school. At Wister Elementary School, he made friends by making people laugh. The other children elected him class president. He was also captain of the baseball and track teams.

Bill developed many of his characters while growing up. Here, he performs with Smokey Robinson.

Making friends and playing sports didn't leave much time for schoolwork. Bill's sixth grade report card says, "William would rather act like a clown than study."

His poor study habits caught up with Bill in high school. He put all his energy into sports and forgot about his books. He was smart enough to earn good grades, but he failed most of his classes. When he couldn't get out of the tenth grade, Bill dropped out of school.

A new start in the Navy

Bill was a good worker, but he didn't have many skills. He soon tired of the dead-end jobs he did find. In 1956, Bill joined the Navy. Four years in the Navy helped him grow up. He earned a high school diploma and worked in a naval hospital. Bill began to think that he could do something useful with his life.

When he was twenty-three, Bill left the Navy to go to college. Temple University's coaches gave Bill a scholarship which paid his college costs. In return, Bill played on Temple's football and basketball teams. He also ran on the track team. Older and wiser now, he earned good grades. Looking ahead, he talked about becoming a physical education teacher.

The scholarship was only good for the school year. During the summer, Bill had to work to support himself.

His first summer job simply paid the bills. But the job
he found after his second year at Temple changed his
life.

*Bill was inducted into the Temple University Hall of Fame in
1984, for his sports efforts in the 1960's.*

CHAPTER TWO

Clowning around pays off

Bill Cosby started the summer of 1961, as a bartender. Before it was over, he was a rising young comedian.

As soon as Bill came to work, the cafe's owner heard a lot of laughing. The customers were breaking up over Bill's stories. The owner knew a good thing when he saw it. He asked Bill to work up a comedy act.

Bill was successful from the start. He did his act at Philadelphia nightclubs and on local television. When school started again, he had to make a tough decision. Working as a comedian meant dropping out of college. Bill decided to take the risk. Making people laugh was what he wanted to do.

The Cosby brand of humor

At first, Bill used other people's jokes. That was okay, because most comedians "steal" from each other. But Bill got his best laughs when he told stories about

Even today, Bill gets his best laughs when he tells stories about his childhood.

his own childhood. His audiences remembered doing the same things when they were kids.

What's funny about a child's life? If you're Bill Cosby, you can find humor in simple things:

"My mother used to get so upset with me. She'd catch me drinking out of the water bottle. 'Did you drink out of this bottle?' 'No, I didn't drink out of the bottle.' 'Then how come there are bread crumbs in the water?!'"

Bill could make any story sound funny, He didn't

Bill has the ability to make any story funny.

just tell stories about Weird Harold. He **became** Weird Harold—and a hundred other characters. In addition to his voices, he put in sound effects. The sound of Dad snoring or Fat Albert running added more humor to his stories.

Hitting the national scene

By 1963, Bill's story of Noah and the Ark had the entire country laughing. As Bill told it, Noah didn't even know what an ark was. But every time the Lord spoke to him, Noah answered, "Ri-i-ight." That one word made the story even funnier.

The Lord: I'm gonna make it rain four thousand days and drown [the world] right out!

Noah: Ri-i-ight! Listen, do this and you'll save water. Let it rain for forty days and forty nights and wait for the sewers to back up!

The Lord: RI-I-IGHT!

Bill's career took off like a skyrocket. His first album, *Bill Cosby Is a Very Funny Fellow, Right!*, became a best seller. He appeared on national television and in *Newsweek* magazine. In 1964, Sheldon Leonard picked Bill to star in *I Spy*. He was the first black to play the lead in a television drama series.

I Spy ran for three years, from 1965 to 1968. Bill's part was that of a tennis coach named Alexander Scott.

Robert Culp played Bill's partner, Kelly Robinson. The two "tennis bums" were really American spies. Bill was so good that he won three Emmy awards as Outstanding Actor in a Dramatic Series. Winning an Emmy in television is like winning an Oscar in the movies.

New projects, new successes

When *I Spy* went off the air, Bill went on to other projects. His first television special won another Emmy. A second comedy-drama series, *The Bill Cosby Show,* ran from 1969 to 1971. Bill played the part of a high school physical education teacher. At that time, blacks had trouble getting work in television. Bill made sure that blacks were hired to work on his show.

"Cos" seldom slowed down. He did live shows at colleges and at Las Vegas, Nevada. Along the way, he made over twenty best-selling albums. Bill also starred in television commercials. He "sold" Coca-Cola, Jell-O, Ford cars, and other products. Ad people say Bill is worth the big money they pay him. He gets results.

A star for all ages

Children's television was also important to Bill. On *Sesame Street,* he taught preschoolers to count. School-

Bill has a warm, loving way with children.

age kids watched him on the *Electric Company.* His warm, loving way with children made him one of America's favorite teachers.

Bill didn't stop there. In 1972, he created a cartoon show called *Fat Albert and the Cosby Kids.* The cartoons make people laugh, but they also teach important lessons. On one show, for example, the gang teased a boy who wears glasses. Later on, they find out that he's the best hitter on the baseball team. "Hey, there's nothing wrong with glasses!" they decide.

Hollywood soon hired Bill to make movies. He made several films, including *Uptown Saturday Night, Let's Do It Again,* and *California Suite.* Bill didn't stay in Hollywood, however. He liked making records, performing in television, and doing live concerts. Most of all, though, he wanted to be with his family.

CHAPTER THREE

A happy family man

Every Thursday night at 8:00 p.m., sixty million Americans sit down to watch television. They're ready to spend a half hour with the Huxtable family.

Many actors would treat the part of Cliff Huxtable as just another acting job. But Bill Cosby plays the part as if he's playing himself. In many ways, he is. Like Dr. Huxtable, Bill centers his life around his family.

The Cosby's family life started in 1963. That's when Bill met Camille Cosby. They didn't have much in common. Camille was a nineteen-year-old university student. Bill was twenty-six, a part-time bartender and comedian. Her family was middle-class; his was poor. Camille's family thought she was making a mistake, but she married Bill in 1964. Not long after, Bill's career moved into high gear with his role in *I Spy*.

Bill and Camille started their family soon after being married. Their first daughter, Erika, was born in 1965. Three more daughters and a son followed: Erinn (1966), Ennis (1969), Ensa (1973), and Evin (1976). Why do all the Cosby children have names starting with

Bill and Camille in a 1966 photo, after he got an Emmy for I Spy.

"E"? Bill says it's so they'll aim for Excellence in their lives.

Twenty years of marriage haven't changed the way Bill feels about his beautiful Camille. He says, "I'm just very, very fortunate that the person I trust the most trusts me, and the person I love the most, loves me." Camille returns his love. It doesn't bother her that she doesn't share his fame. As a friend says, "She would love Bill just as much if he were a teacher."

More than a comedian

Bill does think of himself as a teacher. Even though he dropped out of Temple, he went back to the University of Massachusetts in 1972. For five years, he took courses at night and on weekends. The hard work paid off with a doctorate in education (Ed.D.) The degree means that people should really call him Dr. Cosby. His final project was a book about using the *Fat Albert* show to teach grade school children.

When he finished in 1977, Bill said he would quit show business. He wanted to become a teacher in an inner-city school. Later, he decided that he could help more people by going on with his career. A single teacher reaches thirty students, but a single television show reaches thirty million people! That's why Bill works so hard to put good values into his show. He believes that people who are laughing are also learning.

A man who enjoys his success

Bill's success goes beyond his career and happy family life. His records, commercials, television show, and live shows earn as much as $10 million (US) a year. As Bill says, "I've been poor and I've been rich, and rich is better." Being rich means having fine houses, a jet airplane, and fifteen cars. While he's in New York, he lives in a Manhattan town house. He also owns houses

Bill has been able to enjoy his success.

near Philadelphia and Los Angeles. His main home, however, is near Amherst, Massachusetts. Camille and the children live there in a rebuilt farmhouse.

Money also makes it possible for Bill to enjoy his hobbies. He put the old farmhouse back into perfect condition and filled it with American antiques. At one auction, he paid $95,000 (US) for a set of Tiffany silver. The Cosbys use the silver and the other antiques every day. ''I never want to tell my children they can't sit on this or use that,'' Bill says.

In 1977, Bill earned a Doctor of Education degree from the University of Massachusetts. He says his degree is more important to him than all his show business awards.

CHAPTER FOUR

Is Bill Cosby better than Santa Claus?

A little girl once saw Bill signing his name for his fans. Bill was dressed in a red jogging suit. ''Is that Santa Claus?'' the girl asked. ''No, dear,'' her mother whispered. ''That's Bill Cosby. He's better than Santa Claus!''

Is Bill really better than Santa Claus? Some stars turn out to be rotten people in private life. That's not true of Cosby.

Most of the time, Bill is kind, helpful, and funny. The young actors on his show love him. Lisa Bonet, who plays Denise, goes to him when she needs advice. Macolm-Jamal Warner (Theo) puts it this way: ''He's kind, but tough. . . . If I ever become a father, I'd like to copy his style.''

Don't expect Bill to be smiling all the time, however. At work, he speaks sharply to the other actors if they don't know their lines. Bill doesn't memorize his own lines. He says them the way he thinks will work best.

If the writers don't get a scene right, he tells them to write it again.

Mix love with discipline

Bill wants parents to give their children lots of love and firm rules. He knows that his mother's strong hand and "tender, loving care" kept him out of gangs and drugs. As a result, this loving father never forgets he's also a parent. "I tell [my children] that someday I'm going to leave them a lot of money," he says. "But nobody is getting anything unless they have an education and can understand what to do with that money."

Bill even wrote a how-to book for parents in 1986. Like his show, *Fatherhood* is funny and to the point. "A father must never say, 'Get the kids out of here, I'm trying to watch TV,'" he writes. "If he ever does start saying this, he is liable to see one of his kids on the six o'clock news."

A serious comedian

Some people might think a comedian can't be serious. Bill wouldn't think that's funny. He hires a Harvard professor to check the scripts for his show. The professor looks for scenes that give black people a bad image. Bill also gives his time and money to a number of charities.

In addition, Bill works hard at getting his act exactly right. On stage he looks relaxed, because he knows exactly what he's doing. "If I were a youngster wanting to study stand-up comedy," he says with a smile, "I'd study me!"

To stay in shape, Bill jogs whenever he can. At 48, the old track star still looks like an athlete. He weighs 180 pounds (82 kg) and stands 6'2" (1.88 m) tall. Bill does have one bad habit, however—he smokes long, fat cigars.

Bill has a bad habit. He smokes long, fat cigars.

A moral man remembers his friends

Aside from tobacco, Bill doesn't use drugs of any kind. One of his records, *Bill Cosby Talks to Kids About Drugs,* warns of the dangers of drug abuse. "Every person I have ever known who developed a bad habit spent most of the rest of his life trying to kick it," he says.

Friendship is also important in Bill's life. Sheldon Leonard gave Bill his big break in *I Spy.* Today, Bill says "thanks" by paying Sheldon's restaurant bills when he's in New York. In the same way, Bill won't perform for any casino but Harrah's. He could make more money elsewhere, but Harrah's once helped him out of a sticky tax problem. Sammy Davis, Jr., puts it this way: "His friends are his friends are his friends."

Bill and Harry Belafonte rehearse for a TV show honoring Dr. Martin Luther King.

CHAPTER FIVE

What makes people laugh?

Bill Cosby has his own style of humor. Most comedians tell jokes. Bill tells stories like Mark Twain did. His stories have beginnings and endings. They don't depend on bad words or put-downs. In addition, Bill's humor doesn't depend on his skin color. Other black comedians, such as Richard Pryor and Redd Foxx, tell jokes and stories about being black. The people in Bill's stories could be any color.

Catch Bill's act sometime. He's always the same, whether he's playing Harrah's or taping a new television show. Each story grows out of something that people can remember from their own lives. Bill's version of the story is always wilder and funnier than anyone else's, of course.

Was your first grade like Bill's? The way he tells it, the teacher told the class, "One and one are two." In his six-year-old voice, Bill replies, "Yeah, that's cool, man. One and one are two!" Then he stops, puzzled. "What's a two?" he asks.

Playing all the parts

The people in Bill's stories are bigger than life. When his friend Rudy wears his new sneakers, Rudy doesn't just run fast. Rudy zooms by like a rocket. "What was that?" someone asks. "I don't know," Bill replies, "but it was something fast!"

Adding extra color and excitement to a story is called exaggeration. Bill catches his audience with things that everyone can imagine—then he exaggerates. The stories don't build up to a final "punch line." Instead, Bill rewards his listeners with an almost nonstop series of laughs. If one line doesn't get a laugh, it doesn't matter. The next line surely will.

Bill's stories are full of colorful people. He plays all the parts, changing voices for each character. In a single story, he can be a child, a teenager, and a worried mother. At the same time, he giggles and clowns around. His face and body become part of the action. Bill's face changes to show every emotion a human being can have.

A "childlike comic"

The experts who study humor say that Bill is a visual comedian. He creates "word pictures" that help the audience imagine the scene. A critic once said that a Cosby story is like a cartoon drawn with words.

Bill is a "visual" comedian.

Bill Cosby reaches out to the child in all of us.

30

Comedian Steve Allen has tried to explain Bill's success. Cosby is "our most childlike comic," he says. Steve means that Bill tells stories with the same exaggeration and sound effects a child would use. The child in Bill reaches out to the child in all of us.

Those childlike stories don't just happen. Bill works hard to make his comedy seem fresh and new. When he's not performing, in fact, he often seems rather serious. On a talk show, for example, Bill doesn't tell his usual stories. But even when he's talking about serious matters, the humor still comes through.

Bill doesn't usually watch himself on television. But he feels different about *The Cosby Show*. "I watch every week," he says. "And at the end . . . I find myself with a smile on my face. I really like that family and the feeling they give me."

If the rest of us could stop laughing, we'd surely agree. A reporter once said it for all of us: "I gotta believe that right now he's the most-loved man in America."